Our Eart[illegible] Unique

Keith Ruttle

OXFORD
UNIVERSITY PRESS

Great Clarendon Street, Oxford OX2 6DP

Oxford University Press is a department of the University of Oxford.
It furthers the University's objective of excellence in research, scholarship,
and education by publishing worldwide in

Oxford New York

Auckland Cape Town Dar es Salaam Hong Kong Karachi
Kuala Lumpur Madrid Melbourne Mexico City Nairobi
New Delhi Shanghai Taipei Toronto

With offices in

Argentina Austria Brazil Chile Czech Republic France Greece
Guatemala Hungary Italy Japan Poland Portugal Singapore
South Korea Switzerland Thailand Turkey Ukraine Vietnam

Oxford is a registered trade mark of Oxford University Press
in the UK and in certain other countries

First published 2006

British Library Cataloguing in Publication Data

Data available

ISBN 978-0-19-917948-0

20

Printed in China by Imago

Acknowledgements

The publisher would like to thank the following for permission to reproduce photographs: **p4** NASA, **p5** NASA, **p6** Hubblesite.org, (inset) NASA, **p7**t Corbis/Paul Steel, b Corbis/Roger Ressmeyer, **p8**t Corbis/Onne Van der Wal, b Corbis/Craig Tuttle, **p9**b Corbis/Staffan Widstrand/Zefa, t Classet/OUP, **p10**t Corbis/Paul A Souders, b Corbis/Bill Ross, **p11**t Corbis/Renee Lynn, b Corbis, **p12** Corbis/Gary Braasch, (inset) Corbis/Jonathan Blair, **p13**t Corbis/Louie Psihoyos, b Corbis/Charles Lenars, **p14/15** Corbis, (inset **p14**) Corbis/Massimo Mastrorillo, **p15**l Corbis/Robert Pickett r Corbis, **p16**b Joseph Sohn, **p16/17** Corbis/Brandon D Cole, **p17**l Alamy RF, r Corbis/Roger Ressmeyer, **p18/19** B & C Alexander, **p18**t Corbis, b Alamy RF, **p19**t Corbis/Gahen Rowell, b Corbis/Joel Sartore, **p20/21** Corbis/Charles Philip Cangialosi, **p20** Corbis/Daniel J Cox, **p21**l Corbis/Patricia Fogden, r Corbis/Craig Tuttle, **p22/23** Corbis/Firefly Productions, **p22** Corbis/Tim Davies, **p23**t Corbis RF, b Corbis/Martin Harvey, **p24** Corbis, **p25**t Corbis, bl Corbis/Kennan Ward, br Corbis/Michael De Young, **p26/27** Corbis/Kit Haughton, **p26**l Corbis/Martin Harvey, r Corbis/Torleif Svensson, **p27**t Corbis/Ron Sanford, **p28/29** Corbis/Stephen Frink, **p28** Corbis/Bruce Robison, **p29**t Corbis/Amos Nachoum, b Corbis/Charles Krebs.

Cover photogaph by Classet/OUP

Illustration by: **p30/31** Mark Duffin

Design by Bigtop Design Ltd

Contents

Coming home

Imagine you are an astronaut returning from a mission to Mars. You have left a place where there is no air to breathe or water to drink and where the surface is lashed by ferocious dust storms.

Gradually you see the Earth appearing in front of you. At first you see just a tiny blue dot. Then you start to make out familiar shapes and colours. You see green and brown continents set in blue oceans and huge regions of white polar ice covered with swirling clouds.

You look back towards Mars and remember its barren surface. You had felt lonely there. Now you feel that you are coming home.

Mars looks cold and unfriendly.

Why is the Earth unique?

Earth is unique because every corner of the oceans and continents is filled with life, in millions of different varieties. It is the only place in the universe where life of any kind is known to exist.

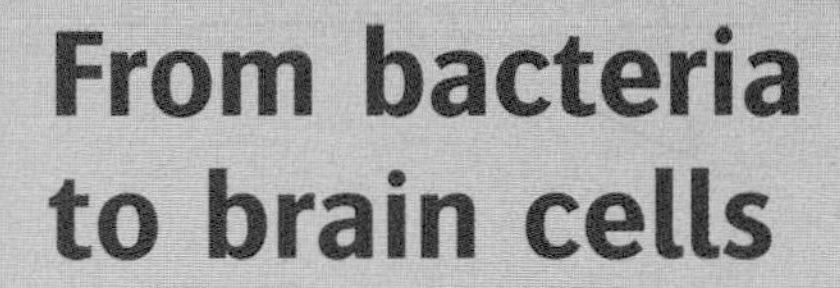

From bacteria to brain cells

The Earth is about 4.5 billion years old. Life is believed to have existed on Earth for over 3 billion years. A billion is 1,000,000,000, so 3 billion years is a very long time indeed.

For several billion years all life consisted of just bacteria and other very simple life forms. Then, about 500 million years ago, many different varieties of living creatures appeared in the seas and oceans. The first plants and animals appeared on land about 400 million years ago. Dinosaurs appeared about 200 million years ago. The earliest ancestors of humans appeared about 4.5 million years ago. Modern humans, who would be recognisable to people today, have lived on Earth for about 100,000 years.

Earth seen from space has been called the 'Blue Marble'.

Why does life exist on Earth?

Life exists on Earth because every part of the Earth's environment is just right to support it. This is not true of anywhere else in the universe that we know about.

Earth is just right!

- Earth's **atmosphere** contains oxygen and other elements in just the right amounts. In particular, it contains only a small amount of carbon dioxide, which is a poisonous gas. The atmosphere of Mars contains a lot of carbon dioxide.
- Earth's climate is just right. For example, in most places on Earth the temperature never varies too much between day and night. On Mars, the difference can be more than 80° Celsius.
- Most importantly, Earth has huge amounts of water in oceans, lakes, rivers and clouds. Water is vital to support life as we know it. There is no water on Mars.

The Martian surface is dry and dusty.

Is there anyone else out there?

Throughout history people have looked up at the stars and wondered whether there might be life somewhere else out there, perhaps in some faraway solar system in a corner of a distant galaxy. The universe is a very big place after all. Scientists now estimate that our own galaxy, called the Milky Way, contains more than 100 billion stars. They also estimate that there are more than 100 billion galaxies in the entire universe!

Water is a prominent feature on Earth.

Looking for life

NASA, the North American Space Agency, has a plan to search for remote planets in our own galaxy, where the conditions for life might exist. The plan is called *Origins* and will last for over 20 years. Giant radio telescopes will look for stars which may have solar systems similar to our own.

Radio telescopes looking for signs of life in distant galaxies.

How can life exist everywhere on Earth?

It never gets as cold on Earth as it does on Mars, but there are some very cold places on Earth, such as Antarctica. There are also some very hot places, such as the Sahara Desert. In fact, many places on Earth are quite different from each other. For example, the bottom of the sea is quite different from the top of a mountain in all sorts of ways.

This starfish lives on the sea floor.

Adaptation

So how is it that plants and animals are able to survive everywhere on Earth in so many different kinds of place?

The answer is that living things always want to find ways of surviving, no matter where they are. Over time, all plants and animals change in ways which make it easier for them to survive in their own surroundings, no matter how hot, cold, dry or wet they are. This is called **adaptation**.

This wildflower meadow has adapted to surviving near these cold mountains.

The colour of these children's skins is a result of adaptation over tens of thousands of years.

Different is good

Adaptation is the reason why living things are different from each other. It is the reason why fish have gills to breathe in water and fins to swim with, and why the arctic fox has white fur in winter rather than brown or black. It is also the reason why some people have dark skin and some people have light skin.

Adaptation has been happening for hundreds of millions of years everywhere on Earth. As a result, there are over a million different types of living thing on Earth that we know about today. However, there may be over ten million other types that we still haven't discovered. Every single one of them has adapted for survival in its own way over millions of years.

Arctic foxes are well camouflaged in the snow.

Species

A grizzly is one species of bear.

Family ties

A living thing is usually described as being a cat, or a bear, or a rose, or whatever. In scientific terms this is called its family. Then you might look closer to see what kind of cat, or bear, or rose, it actually is. This is called its **species**. Every family contains one or more species. Every known living thing on Earth belongs to one species or another.

The name for the variety of all living things on Earth is **biodiversity**. There is a huge amount of biodiversity on Earth.

There are about 100 species of rose.

How do new species happen?

New species come about because of adaptation. For example, some wild cats might need to migrate from one place to another to look for food, but if the new place turns out to be much colder than the old place, then over many generations the wild cats will gradually change to adapt to this colder environment. They might develop longer hair to help keep warm and also change colour to blend into the new landscape. All the changes together will eventually bring about a new species of wild cat. Today, there are 36 species of wild cat living in different parts of the world.

Long hair helps to keep this wild cat warm.

This wild cat's large eyes are a feature that helps it to see and survive in the dark.

Natural selection

Species change and adapt by a process called natural selection. Take the example of the wild cats migrating to a new, colder place. In every generation afterwards, the individual cats which stay warmest by having the longest hair have an advantage in living in that place. These cats will survive more successfully and produce more offspring than others. This process, called natural selection, enables the features most needed for survival to be passed on and improved from generation to generation.

What happens to species?

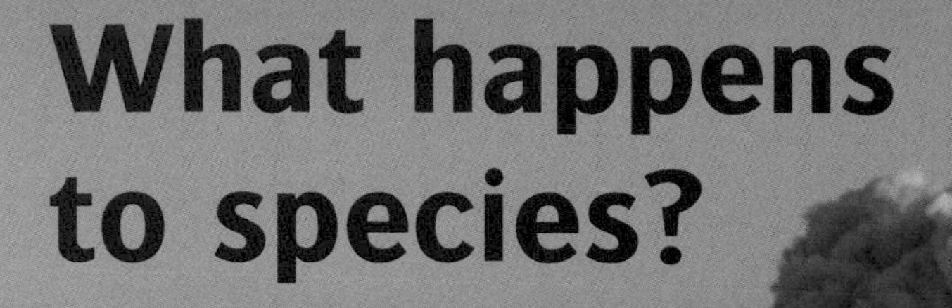

This is a fossil of a pterodactyl – a species that lived over 65 million years ago.

Species come and go

It is natural for new species of plants and animals to appear while other old species disappear. A species usually lives on Earth for between 1 million and 10 million years. When it eventually disappears, it is said to become extinct. Often the only traces left are **fossils** preserved deep inside ancient rocks.

More than 10 million species are living on Earth now, but many more species have lived in the past and have become extinct naturally. Some scientists believe that over 5 billion species have existed since life began! This would mean that well over 99% of species that have ever existed are now extinct.

The volcanic eruption of Mount St Helens, in USA, in 1980, reduced the populations of many species living in the area.

Mass extinctions

Sometimes, many species become extinct in a very short period of time. This is called a mass extinction.

There have been five known mass extinctions in the history of the Earth. The first was over 500 million years ago, when many species disappeared from the seas and oceans. The biggest mass extinction was over 200 million years ago, when more than three-quarters of living creatures suddenly became extinct. The last mass extinction was about 65 million years ago, when the dinosaurs disappeared.

The skull of a Tyrannosaurus rex dinosaur.

It is not known for certain what caused these mass extinctions. Scientists believe that the most likely reason is sudden dramatic changes in the Earth's climate. These could be triggered by violent disasters such as a major volcanic eruption or the Earth being hit by a huge meteorite.

Today, many species are again in danger of becoming extinct all at the same time. This time the main cause is the **impact** of human beings. Human beings affect other species in many ways.

A crater left by a meteorite in Arizona, USA.

Habitats

Where animals live

The place where an animal normally lives and has adapted to survive is called its **natural habitat**. For example, the natural habitat of a polar bear is the snow and ice of the Arctic Circle, not the heat and humidity of the Brazilian rainforest.

An earthworm would probably not survive for long if it were transported suddenly from your local park to a coral reef in the Pacific Ocean. This is because the soil in your local park is the earthworm's natural habitat: a coral reef is not.

This hot and humid Brazilian rainforest produces a lush environment.

A polar bear is extremely well-adapted to living in snow.

The common earthworm, like all living things, has particular needs.

Life support system

The habitat must be able to supply the everyday needs of the animals that live there, such as food, water, warmth and shelter. If the animals' needs are not met, they will need to look urgently for a better habitat.

The sea is a huge habitat where species are constantly competing and co-operating with each other.

Compete or co-operate?

One species of animal often shares the same habitat with other species. In this case, each species has to work out what to do to survive. Their choices are usually either to compete with each other for the same resources, or to co-operate with each other to share the available resources. Sometimes, one species might decide to prey on other species instead. Choices like these are part of the adaptation process. If an animal species makes the wrong choice, then it will probably not survive for long.

Ecosystems

Take any place, such as a forest or a rock pool on the seashore. Now find out everything you can about that place, such as how hot or cold it is, how often it rains there, the types of plants that grow there, and so on. Now identify all the species of insect and animal that live there and see how they survive together. Put all these things together and you have an ecosystem.

A variety of living things lives in a rock pool.

Ecosystems go through cycles, such as the changing of colour of these leaves in autumn.

Big or small

An ecosystem can be very small, such as just one fallen tree inside a wood, or very big, such as the entire Pacific Ocean or even the entire Earth. The size is not important. Ecosystems are simply about looking closely at one particular place to see what lives there and how everything survives.

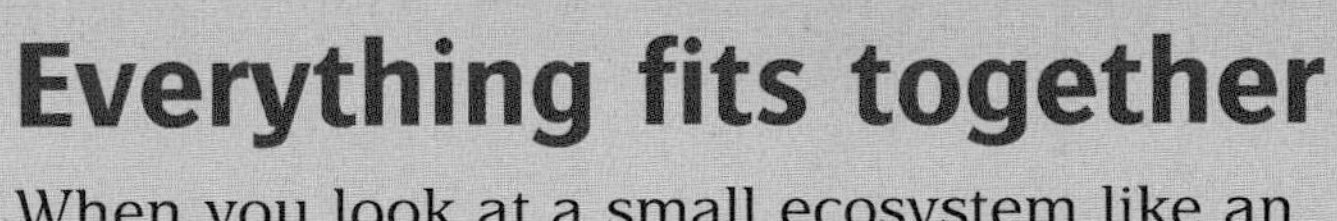

Everything fits together

When you look at a small ecosystem like an old fallen tree, remember that it is always part of something bigger and that everything in the natural environment fits together. The fallen tree is inside a wood, which is inside a park, which is inside a town, and so on.

Try to imagine the whole Earth as one giant ecosystem. Think about how something that happens in one place can have effects far away, even on the other side of the world. For example, think about how a big volcano erupting in one place can affect the weather thousands of miles away, or even change the whole climate of the Earth for several years.

Fallen trees can teem with life.

Volcanoes spew ash into the environment and change the atmosphere around them.

Biomes

A forest is a different kind of place from a desert and an ocean is a different kind of place from an American prairie. In fact, scientists have identified five kinds of place on Earth which are different from each other in important ways. These five kinds of place are called the Earth's **biomes**. They are *forests*, *deserts*, *tundra*, *grasslands* and *oceans*.

Desert

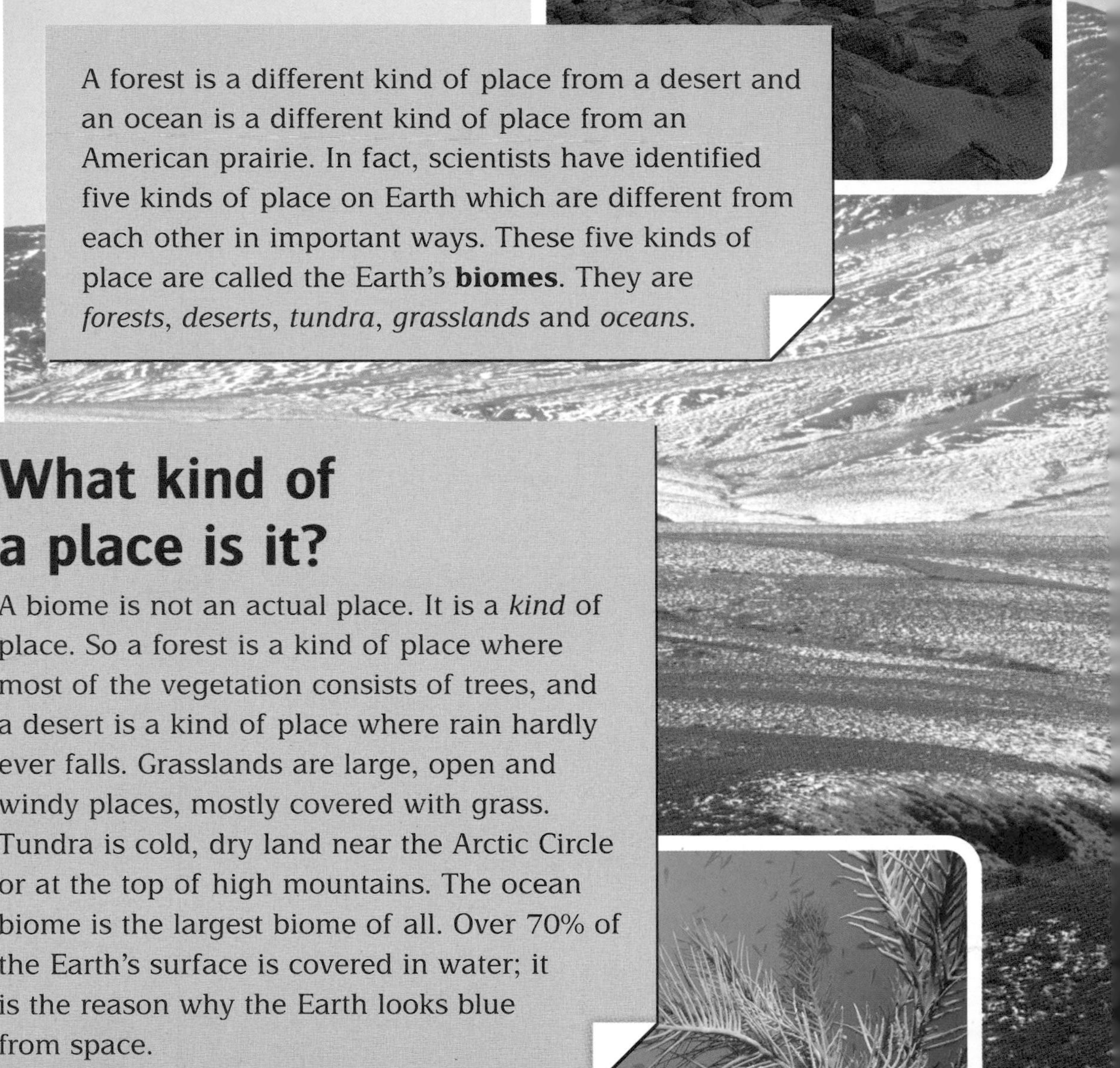

What kind of a place is it?

A biome is not an actual place. It is a *kind* of place. So a forest is a kind of place where most of the vegetation consists of trees, and a desert is a kind of place where rain hardly ever falls. Grasslands are large, open and windy places, mostly covered with grass. Tundra is cold, dry land near the Arctic Circle or at the top of high mountains. The ocean biome is the largest biome of all. Over 70% of the Earth's surface is covered in water; it is the reason why the Earth looks blue from space.

Ocean

Now you can look closely at real places on Earth to see what they are like and which biome they belong to. You can see that the Amazon rainforest is part of the forest biome because it is covered with trees and the Sahara is part of the desert biome because rain hardly ever falls there. You can see that the Great Plains in North America are part of the grasslands biome and the cold land of Alaska is part of the tundra biome.

Forest

Grassland

Every continent on Earth includes various places which belong to different biomes. For example, there are large areas of desert, forest, grassland and tundra in various different regions of North America. Look at the map on page 30 to see where all these places exist.

Tundra

Red pandas live in mountain forests in parts of Asia.

Different kinds of forest

Cold northern places such as Canada have long winters and short summers. Trees, plants and animals living in **coniferous** forests in these places are well adapted to the cold. The trees are mostly sturdy evergreens, such as pine and fir, and the animals often **hibernate** through the long winters when food is scarce. Another name for coniferous forests is **taiga**.

Wolves live in the taiga.

Warmer places further south have shorter winters and longer summers. Forests in these places contain broad-leaved trees such as oak, hazel and maple. They are called **deciduous** forests. Trees in deciduous forests lose their leaves in the autumn, which evergreen trees do not.

Forests in the hot and humid parts of the world near the Equator are called **tropical rainforests**. Here there is no real winter at all. The wintertime is just a bit cooler and rainier than the summertime. Animals, birds and insects living there are often brightly coloured and camouflaged to blend in with their surroundings.

Parts of this scarlet macaw's plumage are similar in colour to the flowers around it.

This rainforest insect is from a species called Copiphora.

How is a forest like a football crowd?

A forest and a football crowd are different in many ways, but are similar in one very important way – both the trees in a forest and the people in a football crowd must breathe to stay alive. Like all animals, people take in oxygen and breathe out carbon dioxide through their lungs. Like all plants, trees take in carbon dioxide and breathe out oxygen through their leaves.

Over one third of the Earth's land is covered by forests. Altogether, the Earth's forests are very important in making sure that the atmosphere always contains just the right amounts of oxygen and carbon dioxide.

Deserts

Extreme temperatures

The hottest place in the world is a place called El Azizia in Morocco, where the temperature has reached 58° Celsius. The coldest place is a place called Vostok in Antarctica, where the temperature has fallen to – 89° Celsius.

What is the connection between El Azizia and Vostok? The answer is that both places are located in the middle of deserts.

A penguin's features allow it to move easily on the Antarctic ice.

You might think that only very hot and sandy places, like the Sahara, can be deserts. In fact, what makes a place a desert is not how hot it is, but how much (or, more precisely, how little) rain falls there. For a place to be a desert, it must have less than 25 centimetres of rain per year. Antarctica has a lot of water, but it is permanently frozen as ice. Very little rain or snow ever actually falls there.

Antarctica is the coldest desert of all and plant and animal life is scarce. The little wildlife there is consists of seabirds, penguins and seals. There are also cold deserts in other parts of the world. For example, the Gobi desert in Asia, being not quite so cold as Antarctica, is rich in wildlife, including wild horses, bears and golden eagles.

Desert shrubs, like this yucca plant, are able to conserve water in their leaves.

Conserve water!

In hot deserts, any rainfall often **evaporates** before hitting the ground. Therefore it is vital that plants and animals in hot deserts **conserve** water in order to survive. The plants growing there are mainly small shrubs which have adapted to avoid losing water through their leaves.

Animals and reptiles often sleep in the shade during the daytime and only become active at night when it is a lot cooler.

This fennec fox is sleeping to conserve energy.

Tundra

Tundra exists in very cold places where only very simple plants like lichens and mosses can live. Larger plants and trees cannot usually survive there because there are not enough **nutrients** in the frozen soil. There are two kinds of tundra: Arctic tundra exists near the North Pole; alpine tundra exists at the top of high mountains around the world.

Frozen solid

In 1977 the well-preserved remains of a baby woolly mammoth were found buried in the tundra in Siberia. Woolly mammoths were big elephant-like creatures which became extinct about 10,000 years ago.

The baby woolly mammoth was preserved because it was buried deep in a layer of frozen soil called **permafrost**. Permafrost never melts. It is the most important **characteristic** of Arctic tundra.

Around the North Pole

The Arctic tundra lies between the coniferous forests of Siberia and Northern Canada, and the North Pole. In the winter, it is frozen and snowy. In the summer, the snow melts and turns the landscape boggy and marshy. There is not very much rainfall.

A peregrine falcon hunting.

Plants and animals in the tundra must be hardy and very well adapted to the winter cold. For example, plants usually have very shallow root systems, as longer roots are not able to penetrate far into the frozen soil. Animals often develop thick layers of fur or fat to keep out the cold. Some animals have adapted by hibernating through the long winters when food is scarce.

Animal species which live in the tundra today include polar bears, caribou, grey wolves, grizzly bears, rabbits and squirrels, as well as birds such as falcons and terns. Tundra birds usually migrate south during the cold winter.

A grizzly bear foraging for food.

A caribou listening for danger.

Grasslands

Wide open spaces

When you think about wildlife in Africa, you might imagine herds of zebra, wildebeest and elephants, and also big cats such as cheetahs and lions. When you think about the great open spaces of the American West, you might imagine herds of bison or maybe families of the famous wild horses called mustángs.

All of these animals live on grasslands, which exist in every continent of the world except Antarctica. Grasslands can cover huge areas of land making a seemingly endless landscape with few trees.

An African bull elephant on the savanna.

A cheetah is easily seen so needs to keep still when stalking prey.

Different names

In Africa, grasslands are known as savanna, and in Northern Asia they are known as steppes. In North America they are called prairies or plains, and in South America they are called pampas.

Grasslands are usually just a bit too wet to become deserts and just a bit too dry to become forests. Any differences between them are mainly caused by the climate in different parts of the world. So the steppe grasslands in Northern Asia are colder and drier than the savanna grasslands in Africa because they are further north.

Huge herds of American bison once roamed the North American plains.

Farming the grasslands

In North America, farmers have discovered that the prairie soil is very **fertile**, especially for crops such as wheat and barley. Today, wheat and barley are grown across huge parts of the prairies and plains in Canada and the American Midwest. Also, many cattle are reared on huge farms called ranches on the prairies of North America and the pampas of South America.

Oceans

Into the abyss

In 1960, a mini-submarine called the *Trieste* reached the deepest point in the ocean for the first time, nearly 11 kilometres (seven miles) down.

Think about the pressure in your ears when you dive just a few metres in the swimming pool. Now imagine how much pressure there must be nearly 11,000 metres down. Imagine, too, how dark and cold it must be at that depth where no sunlight ever reaches. This deep ocean floor is called the abyss.

Angler fish make their own light in the dark abyss.

Strange life

Life began in the oceans billions of years ago. Today, the oceans are filled with thousands of different species, even in the deepest, darkest places where the pressure is enormous.

Some creatures who live in these cold, dark places have adapted to create their own light through chemical reactions. Other creatures have not changed much for millions of years. Some hardy creatures even survive around strange places called vents, which spew out poisonous gases through cracks in the ocean floor.

Near the surface

More familiar species of sharks, whales and fish live closer to the surface where sunlight and warmth do reach. Huge numbers of tiny plants called algae live here too. Like the forests on land, algae take in carbon dioxide from the atmosphere and convert it into oxygen. Scientists calculate that the ocean algae put over 300 *billion* tons of oxygen into the atmosphere every year.

The great white shark is a master of its ocean environment.

Coral reefs

Closer to land, many islands are surrounded by huge barriers called coral reefs. These look like plants but are actually made of millions of tiny animals called coral. Corals have hard shells and also tiny tentacles, which they use to catch food.

Coloured fish, like this canary rockfish, can hide from predators in the coral reef.

Where do you live?

North America

South America

This map shows where each kind of biome exists in the world. Look closely to see which kind of biome you live in. If you live in places like Western Europe or parts of North America, you might be surprised: for example, in most of Britain it is probably difficult to believe that you are really living in a forest biome. The reason is that the map shows how the world would be without the impact of human beings.

- Tundra
- Taiga
- Grassland
- Ocean
- Desert
- Deciduous Forest
- Tropical Rainforest

In reality, over thousands of years, humans have dramatically changed many landscapes all over the world. Many years ago, most of Britain *was* covered in forest. Today almost all the forest has been cut down and replaced with houses and factories, open fields, roads and railways.

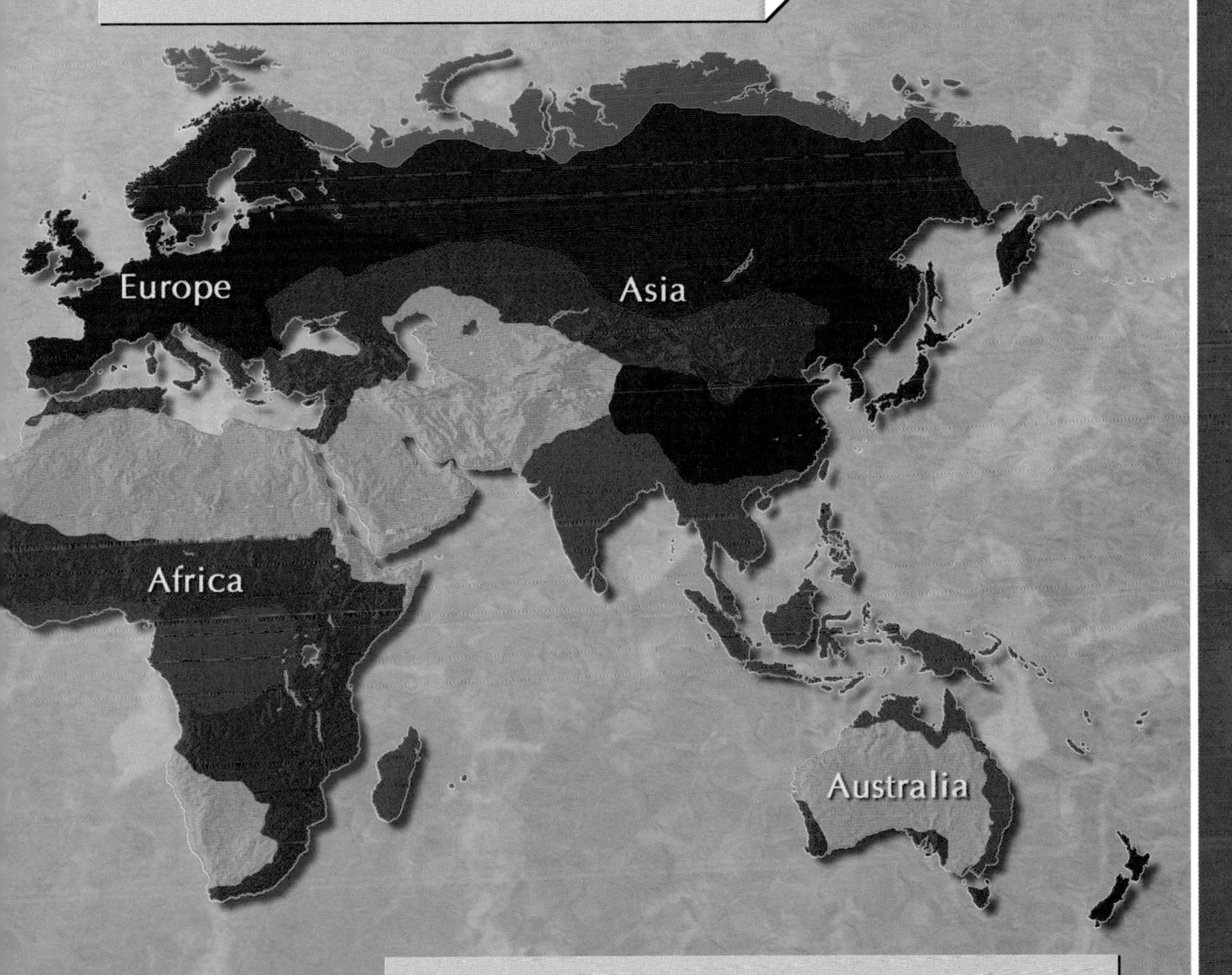

Forests, especially rainforests, are now being cut down at an increasing rate all over the world. Protection of the environment has become a very important issue for people and governments around the world.

Our Earth is unique, after all.

Glossary

adaptation – the way a type of plant or animal changes over generations to become better suited to its surroundings

atmosphere – the mixture of gases that surrounds a planet or star

biodiversity – the variety of all living things on Earth

biomes – the different kinds of natural environments on Earth, consisting of *forests*, *deserts*, *tundra*, *grasslands* and *oceans*

characteristic – a feature which helps to define what something is

coniferous – type of forest in colder regions consisting mainly of evergreens such as pines and firs

conserve – use sparingly, for example water in a hot desert

deciduous – type of forest in warmer regions consisting mainly of broad-leaved trees such as oak, hazel and maple

evaporate – disappear by turning into vapour

fertile – able to produce plenty of healthy crops

fossil – the remains of prehistoric plants and animals preserved inside rocks

hibernate – spend the winter asleep to conserve energy

impact – the effect that one thing has on another, for example, people on the natural environment

natural habitat – the place where an animal normally lives and has adapted to survive

nutrients – elements contained in the soil that plants need to grow

permafrost – permanently frozen layer of soil underneath the Arctic tundra

species – living things of the same type

taiga – another name for coniferous forests

tropical rainforest – type of forest in hot and humid regions near the Equator containing a wide diversity of plant, animal and insect species

Index